Buses, Coaches & Recollecti

Henry Conn

Contents

© Henry Conn 2017

Title page **JEDBURGH** It was in 1963 that bodybuilder Alexander introduced its excellent Y-type body design. Showing off that bodywork in Jedburgh on 24 August is No B92 (AFS 92B), an AEC Reliance new in September 1964, seen in service to Kelso. The day after this view was taken the album *Born to Run* was released, soon to make Bruce Springsteen a rock superstar.

First published in 2017

British Library Cataloguing in Publication Data

A catalogue record for this book is available from the British Library.
ISBN 978 1 85794 517 1

Silver Link Publishing Ltd
The Trundle
Ringstead Road
Great Addington
Kettering
Northants NN14 4BW

Tel/Fax: 01536 330588
email: sales@nostalgiacollection.com
Website: www.nostalgiacollection.com

Printed and bound in the Czech Republic

Acknowledgements

All of the illustrations in this book are from the camera of Bob Gell, without these views and the detailed notes on each, this book would not have been possible. My most sincere thanks to Bob – outstanding.

The PSV Circle Fleet Histories for the operators in this book and a No of issues of *Buses Illustrated* were vital sources of information.

Introduction

In the UK inflation continued to spiral out of control, reaching 24.2%, and the price of petrol increased by nearly 70% in one year. However, the US began to see a reduction, with inflation going down to 9.2%. Both governments used interest rates as a way of trying to control inflation, with the US Federal Reserve at 7.25% and the Bank of England at 11.25%.

Meanwhile, one of the true success stories of modern times was when Bill Gates and Paul Allen create the company Microsoft. The first of the new hobby computers started to appear, including the Altair 8800, and the battle for video recorder standards between VHS and Betamax started.

OPEC agreed to raise crude oil prices by 10%, and oil passed $13.00 a barrel. In the UK the first pipeline to serve the Forties field began pumping North Sea oil, while construction of the Trans-Alaskan pipeline began.

On 11 February Margaret Thatcher became Leader of the Opposition for the Conservative Party; she had been a member and had represented the party in Parliament since 1959, and won the title after successfully challenging the leadership of former Prime Minister Edward Heath, making her the first woman in that role. Later, in 1979, the Conservative Party regained its majority and Margaret Thatcher became the first female Prime Minister of the United Kingdom.

This was also the year that the Vietnam War finally ended. The battle of Ban Me Thuot between South Vietnam and North Vietnam ended on 10 March. North Vietnam had begun a campaign to take the city earlier in the year in an effort to destabilise South Vietnam. On 4 March the offensive was launched, despite a ceasefire having been agreed two years earlier. Ban Me Thuot quickly fell, and it became clear that South Vietnam would have difficulty defending itself against the North in further attacks. By the end of the next month South Vietnam had surrendered to North Vietnam, ending the state of war between them that had existed since 1955. By the end of April North Vietnam had taken Saigon. After realising that it would be impossible to defend the South against the North, the President of the former resigned and his country surrendered unconditionally. The United States' involvement in the war ended on the last day of April, after about 20 years; the last American military members escaped dramatically in helicopters, taking off from the US Embassy in Saigon.

The hit film *Jaws* had its theatrical release in June. It was one of the first blockbuster films and on release became the highest grossing film of all time. It was directed by Steven Spielberg and starred Richard Dreyfuss, Roy Scheider and Robert Shaw. The plot revolved around a killer shark terrorising a small town, and those who were hunting it. It was nominated for several Academy Awards and won three of them. Known for its dramatic score, superior editing and suspenseful premise, *Jaws* is considered by many critics to be one of the greatest films ever made.

General Francisco Franco, the dictatorial leader of Spain, died in November at the age of 82. He had taken power as Spain's head of state in 1939 after his Nationalist forces defeated the Republic during the Spanish Civil War. His early regime was characterised by harsh political oppression, but as he aged more progressive ideas and reforms were allowed. During the Second World War he aligned Spain with the Axis powers, but managed to keep his country only minimally involved in the conflict. After his death the monarchy was restored and King Juan Carlos took power in accordance with Franco's instructions; democracy was established soon after.

Other headlines in the year 1975 included the opening of the Suez Canal for the first time since the Six Day War of June 1967. King Faisal of Saudi Arabia was assassinated, and in India Indira Gandhi was found guilty of electoral corruption.

On 6 June a UK referendum voted 'yes' to stay in the EU, and in the US trade union leader Jimmy Hoffa disappeared, never to be seen again. Motorola obtained a patent for the first ever mobile phone, Microsoft became a registered trademark and, for those with a beard, BIC launched the first disposable razor.

In space, US Apollo and Soviet Soyuz 9 spacecraft linked up in space, and NASA launched the Viking planetary probe toward Mars.

As well as *Jaws*, new films in 1975 included *The Towering Inferno*, *Benji*, *Young Frankenstein*, *The Godfather Part II*, *Funny Lady*, *Murder on the Orient Express*, *The Return of the Pink Panther*, *Tommy* and, my particular favourite, *One Flew over the Cuckoo's Nest*.

In music it was an excellent year, with worthy albums from Aerosmith, Black Sabbath, Chicago, David Bowie, Alice Cooper, The Eagles, Elton John, the very eccentric Kiss, Led Zeppelin, John Lennon, Pink Floyd, Paul Simon, Queen and Bruce Springsteen, and my discovery of the music of ZZ Top.

Enjoy the nostalgia…

 ## Western Scotland

FORT AUGUSTUS Seen in the town on 21 August is Northern No NAC96 (HMS 245), an Alexander-bodied AEC Reliance new in July 1956. At the time this view was taken the coach was on hire to Highland Omnibuses, and was purchased by that company in November; strangely, it was almost immediately withdrawn.

The No 1 single on this day was Can't Give You Anything (But My Love) by the Stylistics.

Above: **FORT AUGUSTUS** Seen on the same day is No BA26 (EWS 115D), an Alexander coach-bodied AEC Reliance new to Scottish Omnibuses in May 1966. It was acquired in July 1973 and remained with Highland until sold for scrap in 1981.

Left: **FORT WILLIAM** In May 1970 Highland acquired the Fort William and Kinlochleven services, and a fleet of 44 buses was transferred from David MacBrayne. One of those transferred was No BA19 (EGB 885C), a Willowbrook-bodied AEC Reliance that had been new in July 1965, and was photographed on 20 August.

On this day NASA launched the Viking 1 planetary probe toward Mars, and after a journey of 10 months and 505 million miles it entered orbit around the planet on 19 June 1976. The lander reached the surface on 20 July, sending back pictures and data until 13 November 1982.

FORT WILLIAM Highland acquired the Oban services of Alexander Midland, and a fleet of 14 buses was transferred in October 1970. Nine of them were Leyland PSUC1/2s, and these were exchanged with Alexander Midland two months later for three AEC Monocoaches and six AEC Reliances, all with Alexander bodywork. Also seen on 20 August is No B80 (RMS 739), one of the AEC Reliances new to Alexander in April 1961; it was sold for scrap in September 1976.

FORT WILLIAM Working a local service from Glen Nevis to Fort William on the same day is No B45 (XGD 776), a Park Royal/Roe-bodied AEC Reliance new to MacBrayne in August 1959 and transferred to Highland in May 1970. It was sold for scrap a little over a year after this view was taken.

OBAN Transferred to Western SMT from MacBrayne on 4 October 1970 were four buses together with services in the Tarbet, Inveraray and Ardrishaig areas. Standing in the centre of this view at Oban on 16 August is Western SMT No ME2 (HGA 985D), a Willowbrook-bodied Bedford VAS1 new to MacBrayne in July 1966. The Excelsior coach (left) is HRU 706N, a Plaxton-bodied Ford R1114 new in April 1975, while NTU 187L on the right is also a Plaxton-bodied Ford R1114 new to Shearings in May 1973.

The day before this view was taken the 'Birmingham Six', Hugh Callaghan, Paddy Joe Hill, Gerry Hunter, Richard McIlkenny, Billy Power and Johnny Walker, were sentenced to life imprisonment after being convicted of the murder of 21 people in the bombings of the Mulberry Bush and Talk of the Town pubs in Birmingham on 21 November 1974. After a 16-year campaign, which showed that the police had coerced their confessions and had mishandled evidence, their convictions were overturned in 1991.

OBAN About to work the short 1-mile journey to Ganavan Sands, an excellent beach north of Oban, is No T62 (SST 262K), one of a batch of 12 Willowbrook-bodied Ford R192s that were purchased new by Highland in June and July 1972. After a relatively short service life all of the batch had been withdrawn by February 1983.

CRAIGNURE is the main ferry port on the east coast of on the Island of Mull, and bus services go from the village to Tobermory (north) and Fionnphort (west). At the bus park in Craignure on 17 August is Highland No CD42 (372 FGB), a Duple-bodied Bedford VAS1 new to MacBrayne in 1962 and transferred to Highland in April 1970. Bowman of Craignure acquired the vehicle in April 1976 and it remained in that fleet until September 1982.

FIONNPHORT The MacBrayne bus operations on Mull and a fleet of 16 Bedford buses were transferred to Highland on 27 November 1971. Standing at Fionnphort, also on 17 August, is Highland No CD81 (MGB 285E), a Plaxton-bodied Bedford SB5 new in May 1967; it was later acquired by Peace of Kirkwall, Orkney, in November 1980. Fionnphort is the base for the ferry service to Iona, and from the village the entire east side of that island can be seen, including Iona Abbey.

The excellent Rod Stewart album Atlantic Crossing *was soon to be No 1. Listen to* Stone Cold Sober, *one of the least well-known songs on the album – there's a superb guitar solo at the end reminiscent of Lynyrd Skynyrd.*

Below: **FIONNPHORT** On the same day we see USB 159M, a Willowbrook-bodied Ford R1014 new to Bowman in August 1973.

Above: **FIONNPHORT** The Bowmans, farmers at Scallastle near Craignure, began the Craignure to Fionnphort bus service in 1956 on a one-return-journey-a-day basis, connecting with the Sound of Mull mail steamer, with the driver having to sleep over at the Iona ferry end of the route each weeknight. After 1964, with the arrival of the car ferry and several daily sailings to and from Oban, frequencies were increased and a substantial programme of coach tours was operated from Craignure in connection with the comings and goings of the ferry. By 1980 Highland Omnibuses had withdrawn from Mull, and its Tobermory to Craignure route also passed to Bowmans. In June 2013 Bowman Tours Limited, together with ten vehicles, was purchased by West Coast Motors of Campbeltown and both the tour operations and the Tobermory and Fionnphort bus routes are now operated by that company. Standing at Fionnphort on 17 August is RSB 77K, a Willowbrook-bodied Ford R192 new to Bowman in July 1972.

Tayside and Central Scotland

Above right: **PITLOCHRY** A short drive from the town, along a winding tree-lined road hugging the River Tummel, lies the Queen's View. This famous vantage point looks out over one of the most iconic panoramas in Scotland, directly to the west along Loch Tummel, from where, on a clear day, you can sometimes see the mountains surrounding Glencoe by the west coast. A popular destination since Victorian times, it is often thought that the location was named after Queen Victoria who did, in fact, visit in 1866. However, it is more widely believed to have been named after Queen Isabella, the 14th-century wife of Robert the Bruce, who used the spot as a resting place on her travels. In the car park at Queen's View is No MW290 (SMS 830H), a Duple-bodied Bedford VAS5 new in May 1970 and sold to Reynolds of Gwespyr in February 1980.

Right: **ABERFELDY** In service to Pitlochry on 10 August is MPD235 (TWG 589), an Alexander coach-bodied Leyland PSUC1/2 new in July 1962. It has been modified for one-person operation, but retains coach seats; it would be sold for scrap in February 1978.

On this day former US President Richard Nixon signed a contract with TV journalist David Frost agreeing to answer any questions posed in four sessions of 90 minutes each. In return, Nixon would receive $700,000. The meetings would later be the subject of the film Frost/Nixon.

Above right: **DUNKELD** In service to Aberfeldy on 15 August is No MPD198 (OMS 274), an Alexander coach-bodied Leyland PSUC1/2. A few months later, in December 1975, the coach was sold to a dealer for scrap.

Above: **DUNDEE** During 1955 Dundee Corporation took delivery of 35 MCCW-bodied Daimler CVG6s, purchased for tram replacement. Remarkably, when the Corporation became Tayside Regional Council in May 1975, 33 of the batch were transferred, and representing that batch is No 197 (ETS 977). When this view was taken on 11 August, No 197 was still in Dundee Corporation livery.

Left: The next three photographs were also taken on 11 August, and in High Street, working a local town service to Letham, is No MRD142, (RWG 365), an ECW-bodied Bristol LD6G new in April 1961.

On this day 78% of British Leyland Motor Corporation, the UK's largest motor manufacturer, came under the control of the British Government.

Left: **PERTH** Also working a Perth local service to Muirton is No MRF13 (HWG 512E), an Alexander-bodied Daimler CRG6LX new in January 1967 and sold for scrap in June 1982.

Below: **PERTH** Heading north to Stanley is WPT 797, belonging to F.A. & C. McLennan of Spittalfield. A Plaxton Derwent-bodied Ford R192, it was new to Trimdon Motor Services Limited in October 1967. It passed to Jersey Motor Transport in June 1971, where it remained until it was repurchased by Trimdon in December. Earnside Coaches of Glenfarg acquired the bus in early 1975, but it was not operated, and was acquired by McLennan in June, and there it remained until its sale to Moncrieff of Leuchars as a non-PSV. The bus was last licensed by McIntyre of Colliston in August 1990, and sold for scrap a few months later.

ST ANDREWS The next four views were all taken on 14 August. In South Street, heading for Falkland, is Cupar-allocated No FPD195 (OMS 271), an Alexander coach-bodied Leyland PSUC1/2 new to Alexander in July 1960. Less than a month later the coach was sold to Muir of Kirkcaldy, where the vast majority of Fife buses were scrapped.

Right: **ST ANDREWS** Apparently on hire to 'The Glen' Old Boys Club is Fife No FT4 (HSF 549N), a Duple coach-bodied Ford R1014 new in January 1975.

Below left: **ST ANDREWS** As seen here, the Albion Viking VK43AL had the engine, a Leyland 400, longitudinally mounted partially under the floor at the rear. Interestingly, the linkage from the manual gearstick to the Albion five-speed gearbox passed diagonally along the entire length of the bus – 30 feet. This is Fife No FNV40 (MXA 640G), with Alexander coach bodywork new in July 1969.

Below right: **ST ANDREWS** Also on hire to 'The Glen' Old Boys Club is No FPE42 (WXA 942M), an Alexander-bodied Leyland PSU3/3R new to Fife in November 1973. There seem to be a lot of ladies on the Old Boys tour!

1975
No 1 Records

January
Lonely this Christmas   *Mud*
Down, Down   *Status Quo*
Ms Grace   *Tymes*
February
January   *Pilot*
Make me smile (Come up and see me)   *Steve Harley &*
                                          Cockney Rebel

March
If   *Telly Savalas*
Bye, Bye Baby   *The Bay City Rollers*
April
              Bye, Bye Baby - stays at No 1
May
Oh Boy   *Mud*
Stand by your man   *Tammy Wynette*
June
Whispering Grass   *Windsor Davies & Don Estelle*
I'm not in love   *10 cc*
July
Tears on my pillow   *Johnny Nash*
Give a little love   *The Bay City Rollers*
August
Barbados   *Typically Tropical*
Can't give you anything (But my love)   *Stylistics*
September
Sailing   *Rod Stewart*
October
Hold me close   *David Essex*
I only have eyes for you   *Art Garfunkel*
November
Space oddity   *David Bowie*
D.I.V.O.R.C.E   *Billy Connolly*
Bohemian Rhapsody   *Queen*
December
Bohemian Rhapsody - *stays at No 1*

CRIEFF Alexander Midland purchased new 44 Alexander-bodied Albion Lowlander LR1s, which were delivered in 1963 and 1964. Standing in Crieff on 10 August is No MRE40 (VWG 378), which was new in December 1963 and was sold for scrap in July 1978. I think the Albion behind looks so much smarter with just the addition of the silver wheel rings.

Below: **CALLANDER** Also in the car park that day was, on the left, No MRD174 (VWG 354), an ECW-bodied Bristol FLF6G new in May 1963. The 15 ECW-bodied Bristol VRTs that were purchased new by Midland between February and April 1970 were not a success and were all exchanged for 15 ECW-bodied Bristol FLF6Gs from Eastern National between August and October 1971. On the right is No MRD196 (RVW 392D), which was new to Eastern National in July 1966. No MRD174 was sold in December 1978 and No MRD196 a year later.

Above: **CALLANDER** railway station was closed under the 'Beeching Axe' on 5 November 1965, the track through the station was lifted in late 1968, and some demolition work was carried out; the track to the west of the station had been lifted in early 1967. The station building itself was demolished in the spring of 1973, and the site is now a car park, though a small section of the down platform still exists. Standing in the station car park on 12 August is Alexander Midland No MRE4 (TWG 555), an Alexander-bodied Albion LR1 new in January 1963. It was acquired by Highland in December 1975, received fleet number AL47 and remained in the fleet until December 1977, when it was sold for scrap.

On this day John Walker of New Zealand became the first person to run a mile in less than 3 minutes 50 seconds in Gothenburg, Sweden.

Edinburgh

ST ANDREW SQUARE All the following pictures in and around St Andrew Square bus station were taken on 2 August. Seen here approaching the bus station is Lothian Transport No 674 (ASC 674B), an Alexander-bodied Leyland PD3/6 new to Edinburgh Corporation in August 1964. No 674 was sold to a dealer in Swansea in December 1976, then acquired and licensed by D Coaches of Morriston in April 1977, where it remained until June 1981.

In early August 1975 a gallon of petrol cost 72 pence, the inflation rate was a mind-boggling 24.2%, and interest rates were 11.25%.

Right: **ST ANDREW SQUARE** The final batch of ECW-bodied Bristol FLF6Gs purchased new by Fife in May and June of 1967, HXA 400E to 417E, were built to the extended 31ft 6in length. They were also the last Bristol FLFs built for any member of the Scottish Bus Group; sadly all were withdrawn in 1981. This is No FRD213 (HXA 413E), which was allocated to the Aberhill depot.

ST ANDREW SQUARE A large batch of Alexander dual-purpose-bodied AEC Reliances were delivered between March and June 1960. In its final few months of service, abandoned by all, is No B788 (USC 788).

ST ANDREW SQUARE Delivery of 25 ECW-bodied Bristol FLF6Gs was brought forward from 1967 by several months to coincide with the opening of a new depot in Dalkeith. They were numbered AA207 to 231 (GSG 207D to 231D), and all had been delivered by November 1966. They were all allocated to Dalkeith for their working lives, apart from a handful that passed to Bathgate towards the end of their service life. Leaving St Andrew Square bus station for Birkenside is No AA213 (GSG 213D).

ST ANDREW SQUARE Eastern Scottish preferred Bedfords for its lightweight buses, whereas other SBG companies preferred Ford. The first 20, Nos C232 to C251 (HSF 232E to 251E), were Bedford VAM5s with Alexander bodywork and were delivered in May and June 1967. They spent their first few months working on urban routes in Edinburgh, then all were transferred to the Border depots. Interestingly, seen here on the right is No C250 (HSF 250E) working to Birkenside, a Dalkeith-operated route, but the depot code after the fleet number, 'J', indicates that the bus was allocated to Berwick-upon-Tweed. Standing alongside is No AC520 (BSG 520L), an Alexander-bodied Bedford YRQ allocated at this time to Edinburgh New Street depot.

ST ANDREW SQUARE The final new Leyland PSU5A/4R Leopards to enter the fleet of Eastern Scottish were Nos XH375 to XH377 (HSG 564N to 566N), new in March 1975. They were Alexander M-type London coaches, 12 metres long with Pneumocyclic transmission – I think a classic-looking coach. No XH375 is seen here on Platform E in the bus station, and within days it was acquired by Northern.

In the infamous SBG/NBC Bristol Lodekka/ Bristol VRT swap, Eastern Scottish received Bristol FLF6Gs from a number of NBC companies. Some of them, as illustrated in this view of No AA991 (KDL 145F), had Tilling T-type destination displays. No AA991 had come from Southern Vectis, retaining the T-type destination, and was allocated to Dalkeith depot for its service life.

Right: **ST ANDREW SQUARE** In the early morning of 2 August, just arrived overnight from the East Midlands (left), is Barton No 1215 (LAL 317K), a Plaxton-bodied Leyland PSU3B/4R new in May 1972. Interestingly, when sold by Barton it was acquired by Moffat & Williamson of Gauldry, Fife, and remained in Scotland when Meffan of Kirriemuir acquired it in August 1984. Alongside No 1215 is an Alexander-bodied Bedford YRQ demonstrator, WXE 264M, which was on long-term loan to Eastern Scottish from December 1973.

ST ANDREW SQUARE Leaving the bus station (with a stunningly informative destination display!) is United No 1154 (OPT 994K), a Plaxton-bodied AEC Reliance new to Gillett of Quarrington Hill in August 1971, and acquired when United took over Gillett's business in November 1974. Also about to leave with another informative destination display is No 6079 (SHN 79L), an ECW-bodied Bristol RE new to United in 1973.

Right: **ST ANDREW SQUARE** Between March and June 1958 20 ECW coach-bodied Bristol MW6Gs were delivered, RSC 622 to 641. All the Bristol MW coaches were downgraded to dual-purpose between 1963 and 1965 and received fibreglass destination screens at Marine Works, as illustrated here. This is No ZA623, allocated to Musselburgh depot, leaving for North Berwick and still looking very smart for its age.

Below: **ST ANDREW SQUARE** An iconic view of a number of Alexander M-type coaches ready for boarding.

Just a few nights later, the Usher Hall in Lothian Road hosted Hawkwind on their 'Warrior on the Edge of Time' tour, the final tour of Stacia, their 'interpretive dancer'. Stacia left after the tour, which signalled the end of an era for Hawkwind.

ST ANDREW SQUARE In 1959 29 Park Royal dual-purpose-bodied AEC Reliances were delivered. The first 20 featured head cushions, whereas the remainder, which included No B701 (SWS 710) seen here, did not. This may be the last view of this bus in service; note also the paper destination sticker, something very regularly used by Eastern Scottish.

1975 Arrivals & Departures

Births

Edith Bowman	*disc jockey*	15 January
Keith Gillespie	*footballer*	18 February
Gary Neville	*footballer*	18 February
Drew Barrymore	*actress*	22 February
Robbie Fowler	*footballer*	9 April
David Beckham	*footballer*	2 May
Enrique Inglesias	*singer*	8 May
Jonah Lomu	*rugby player*	12 May
John Higgins	*snooker player*	18 May
Jamie Oliver	*chef*	27 May
Angelina Jolie	*actress*	4 June
Jill Halfpenny	*actress*	15 July
Kate Winslet	*actress*	5 October
Ronnie O'Sullivan	*snooker player*	5 December
Tiger Woods	*golfer*	30 December

Deaths

P.G. Wodehouse	*English writer*	(b. 1881)	14 February
Susan Hayward	*actress*	(b. 1917)	14 March
Aristotle Onassis	*shipping magnate*	(b. 1906)	15 March
King Faisal of Saudi Arabia	*actor*	(b. 1906)	25 March
William Hartnell	*actor*	(b. 1908)	23 April
Eamon de Valera	*3rd Irish President*	(b. 1882)	29 August
Haile Selassie 1	*Ethiopian Emperor*	(b. 1892)	27 September
Graham Hill	*racing driver*	(b. 1929)	29 November

ST ANDREW SQUARE On hire to Eastern Scottish for City sightseeing tours is Ribble No 1042 (UTF 722M), a Duple-bodied Leyland PSU3B/4R new in May 1974. In contrast, standing next to it is No AA606 (OWS 606), one of the long-lived ECW-bodied Bristol LD6Gs new in 1957. Furthest away is No AA876 (YWS 876), an ECW-bodied Bristol FLF6LX new in April 1962; at this time it was allocated to Peebles and is soon to take up service to Galashiels, quite a long journey of 33 miles for a double-deck bus!

HAWORTH Arriving on 28 June is West Yorkshire No 1735 (2026 YG), an ECW-bodied Bristol FS6B new in December 1961.

A few days before this view was taken a coroner's court jury returned a verdict of wilful murder, naming Lord Lucan as the murderer, in the inquest on Sandra Rivett, the nanny who had been found dead at his wife's London home 7 months previously; the whereabouts of Lord Lucan have remained a mystery to this day.

YORK Looking down from the City Wall, this is York West Yorkshire No 3964 (OWR 552M), an ECW-bodied Bristol VRT/SL6G new in January 1974.

The No 1 single on this day was Tammy Wynette with Stand by your Man.

1975 Happenings (1)

January
- Watergate verdict finds defendents John Ehrlichman, John Mitchell and Harry Haldeman guilty of cover up.
- Work abandoned by Britain on the latest Channel Tunnel on financial grounds.
- Dr Donald Coggan becomes 101st Archbishop of Canterbury.
- Donald Nielsen abducts Leslie Whittle from Shropshire home.

February
- Margaret Thatcher succeeds Edward Heath as Conservative Party leader
- Moorgate Tube crash kills 41 people
- New £10 note issued by the Royal Mint featuring the H M The Queen on the front and Florence Knightingale on the reverse.
- P.G. Wodehouse dies at the age of 93 in Remsenburg, USA.

March
- Charlie Chaplin knighted by the H M The Queen at Buckingham Palace on a rare visit to the UK.
- The USSR and the USA carry out underground nuclear tests.
- Leslie Whittle found dead at the bottom of a drain shaft.
- Colour TV broadcasts begin in Australia.

HALIFAX Leaving Crossfield bus station for Bradford on 28 June is West Yorkshire PTE No 2605 (HUA 556N), an MCW-bodied Scania BR111DH new in April 1975. West Yorkshire purchased new 95 Scanias between 1975 and 1977, and they were known to have a lively performance and a smooth ride due to their air suspension. However, they were also known for their thirst for fuel and, over a short time, severe corrosion of the body structure. It was due to this that by 1985 all 95 examples in the WYPTE fleet had been withdrawn. In the background is former Halifax Corporation No 67, a Weymann-bodied Leyland PD2/37 new in 1966.

HALIFAX Leaving the bus station on the same day on route 8 to Leeds is WYPTE No 3260 (OJX 60K), a Plaxton Derwent dual-purpose-bodied AEC Reliance new to Halifax B fleet in 1971.

The excellent I'm Not in Love by 10CC was the No 1 single on this day.

HALIFAX WYPTE No 2352 (XAK 352L) is a Daimler CRL6, new to Bradford City Transport in 1972 with an Alexander body. Following a fire, it was rebodied as seen here with a low-height Northern Counties body and transferred to Halifax, where it was re-engined with a Gardner 6LX to match the rest of the Halifax Daimlers.

Greater Manchester

SWINTON The Lancastrian Hall and Central Library building, overlooking the A6 in Swinton, is in a familiar 1960s style using concrete slabs and pebbledash. Passing the library on 15 October is GMPTE No 3148 (MRJ 302F), an MCCW-bodied Leyland PDR1/1 new to Salford City Transport in 1968.

Two days before this view was taken Norton Villiers, which produced motor cycles in Wolverhampton, closed down with the loss of 1,600 jobs after being declared bankrupt.

Right: **SWINTON** Near the same spot on the same day, passing the Bulls Head in Chorley Road, is GMPTE No 67 (XNA 405L), a Duple-boded Leyland PSU3B/4R new to the South East Lancashire & North East Cheshire PTE (SELNEC) in May 1973.

At the end of October Queen released one of the most iconic singles ever, Bohemian Rhapsody, which became the UK's third highest-selling single of all time.

Far Right: **LEIGH** Corporation Transport needed low-bridge or low-height double-deckers because of low bridges in its operating area and the low headroom at its depot. Before purchasing AEC Renowns between 1963 and 1967, Leigh took delivery of Dennis Lolines or low-bridge Leyland Titans. Leigh Corporation No 22 (722 ATE) was a Leyland Titan PD2/20 with East Lancashire low-bridge body new in 1957. It passed to SELNEC PTE on 1 November 1969, was renumbered 6952 in the Northern Division series, and is seen at Leigh bus station in King Street, also on 15 October, after it had passed to Greater Manchester PTE. I think at the time this view was taken that there was a cinema, The Regal, to the right of this view, and the film showing could well have been *Farewell My Lovely* with Robert Mitchum as private eye Phillip Marlowe.

Right: **LEIGH** Corporation switched to single-deck East Lancashire-bodied Leyland PSU4/2Rs for its final deliveries in 1968 before the setting up of the GMPTE. In Leigh bus station on that October day, in full GMPTE livery, is No 6060 (HTJ 131F); this East Lancashire-bodied Leyland Leopard was a popular combination with many of the Lancashire municipal fleets.

Above: **WIGAN** Working a local service to Beech Hill, also on 15 October, is GMPTE No 3232 (HEK 707), a Massey-bodied Leyland PD3A/2 new to Wigan in 1961.

Above right: **WIGAN** Northern Counties Motor & Engineering Company Limited was founded in Wigan in 1919 by Henry Lewis, and the Lewis family remained owners of the company until it was bought out more than 70 years later. As was common at the time, early products were bodywork for private automobiles. By the early 1920s that work had ceased and the manufacture of bodywork for service buses commenced, in both single-deck and double-deck form – very few coaches were produced. On the forecourt of Northern Counties in Wigan on 15 October, awaiting delivery, is GMPTE No 7597 (LNA 250P), a Leyland AN68A/1R.

Right: **BOLTON** In Bolton bus station on 14 April is No 6031 (LDK 831G), one of a batch of four Willowbrook-bodied Daimler SRG6LXs delivered to Rochdale in September 1968.

The No 1 single was Bye Bye Baby by the Bay City Rollers, which had unfortunately replaced the excellent Steve Harley single Make Me Smile (Come Up And See Me)!

BURY A number of the Leyland Nationals delivered in 1974 were white, and in Bury on 14 April is No 1316 (XVU 383M) in that livery.

A week before this view was taken Ritchie Blackmore played his last concert with Deep Purple in Paris and formed his own group, Rainbow.

1975 Happenings (2)

April
- Vietnam War ends as the Capital - Saigon falls to North Vietnamese troops.

May
- England beat Scotland 5-1 at Wembley in the home internationals
- Flixborough Inquiry published. Finds bypass pipe failed due to unforeseen lateral stresses.

June
- The Suez Canal is re-opened by Egypt's President Sadat
- British people vote in first ever referendum and decide (67.2% in favour) to stay in the EEC
- Inquest finds, in his absence, Lord Lucan guilty of murdering nanny Sandra Rivett.
- First North Sea oil from the British sector comes ashore at BP's Refinery on the Isle of Grain
- First live radio broadcast from House of Commons

July
- American *Apollo* and Russian *Soyuz* space craft dock in space - astronauts shake hands!
- American president Gerald Ford visits the Nazi Concentration Camp at Auschwitz.

August
- The *Birmingham Six* are wrongfully sentenced to Life Imprisonment.
- The ailing British Leyland is nationalised.

Below: **STOCKPORT** In the background of this view, also taken on 14 April, is Stockport railway viaduct, standing 33.85 metres high and said to contain some 11 million bricks. It was designed by G. W. Buck to carry the Manchester & Birmingham Railway across the centre of the town in the valley of the River Mersey. Opened in 1842 with services running via Crewe, it enabled travellers from Stockport to reach London; the viaduct was widened in 1889 to accommodate four tracks, and in 1989 was floodlit and cleaned in a £3 million restoration project. No 7125 (XJA 516L), a Park Royal-bodied Leyland AN68/1R new in 1972, is flanked by Nos 111 and 117 (HNE 635N and HNE 647N), Leyland Nationals new in March and April 1975.

Above: **STOCKPORT** The Transport Act of 1968 set up the South East Lancashire & North East Cheshire (SELNEC) Passenger Transport Executive, and on 1 November 1969 the PTE absorbed 11 local authority undertakings and was given the responsibility of coordinating the stage carriage services within its area. More than half of North Western's stage services were operated in the SELNEC PTE area, and in 1971 it was agreed that the PTE would take over the stage carriage services of the North Western Road Car Company in the PTE operating area, which took effect from 1 January 1972. Both buses seen here, also on 14 April, are Bristol REs; on the right is No 327 (NJA 327H), bodied by Alexander and new in 1969, while No 284 (KJA 284F) was bodied by Marshall and new in 1968.

STOCKPORT On the left in Mersey Square on the same day is No 4167 (DDB 167C), an Alexander-bodied Daimler CRG6LX new to North Western in 1965. On the right is No 5869 (HJA 969E), a Neepsend-bodied Leyland PD2/40 new to Stockport in 1967. The Neepsend company, named after the area in Sheffield where the bodybuilder's factory was located, lasted only for around four years before the factory was closed.

1975 Happenings (3)

September
- The Provisional IRA bomb London's Hilton Hotel killing two and injuring more than sixty.
- The Spaghetti House siege in Knightsbridge, London ends after six days with both robbers and hostages physically unharmed.

October
- Bill Clinton marries Hilary Rodham.
- Bomb explodes outside central London's Green Park tube station.
- Peter Sutcliffe, *The Yorkshire Ripper* commits murder for the first time.
- Prince Juan Carlos named Spanish Head of State as Francisco Franco's health deteriorates.

November
- First North Sea oil pipeline from Cruden Bay to Grangemouth is opened officially by H M The Queen
- Australian Prime Minister Gough Whitlam dismissed by Sir John Kerr the Govenor General. Malcolm Fraser appointed.
- Ross McWhirter is murdered outside his Enfield home after offering reward for information leading to the arrest of suspected terrorists

December
- The UK's *Sex Discrimination act* becomes law
- Icelandic North Sea patrol fires on unarmed British fishing vessel - the *Cod War* starts

NOTTINGHAM The Nottingham pictures were all taken on 12 June, and neck and neck with a Series 1 Jaguar E-Type on that day is Nottingham No 65 (65 RTO), an NCME-bodied Daimler CRG6LX new in September 1963; it would pass to Theobald of Long Melford for further service in December 1977. The Jaguar E-Type Series 1 cars, which are by far the most valuable, essentially fall into two categories: those made between 1961 and 1964, which had 3.8-litre engines and non-synchromesh transmissions, and those made between 1965 and 1967. The latter had engine size and torque increased by around 10%, a fully synchronised transmission, new reclining seats, an alternator in place of the prior generator, an electrical system switched to negative earth, and other modern amenities, while still keeping the same classic Series 1 styling.

NOTTINGHAM Leaving Victoria bus station, working the X42 express to Derby, is Trent No 248 (ECH 248C), a Willowbrook dual-purpose-bodied Leyland PSU3/3R new in May 1965 and still looking smart in its non-NBC livery.

On the previous day the UK became an oil-producing nation when the first crude oil was pumped into the tanker Theogennitor from a well located 180 miles off the coast of Scotland in the Argyll oilfield.

458/ETO.C & 407 BTU. B/BEING DILERED TO BILBOROUGH
DEPOT. (BEING TAILEN INTO BILBOROUGH DEPOT STOCK)
AND 128 MTO.F ON THE 45 ROUTE TO WOLLATON PARK
D. PURPLE 19.12.2018)

NOTTINGHAM Heading for Parliament Street depot in Derby Road is No 458 (ETO 458C), an MCCW-bodied Leyland PDR2/1 new in October 1965. Following fire damage in February 1974 No 458 was rebuilt by NCME at the front, incorporating 1966-style top-deck front windows and domes – compare the rebuild with No 407 running behind.

AND BARTON/ROBIN HOOD COACH
ON THE 5 ROUTE TO LONG EATON
ONLY
D. PURPLE 19.12.2018)

NOTTINGHAM Working on route 44 in Derby Road is No 176 (ETO 176L), a Willowbrook-bodied Daimler CRG6LX new in May 1973.

The No 1 single was Whispering Grass by Windsor Davies and Don Estelle, both well known for their roles in It Ain't Half Hot Mum, which ran for eight series between 1974 and 1981.

Below: **LEICESTER** The Leicester pictures were taken on 11 January, and standing in front of the Midland Red depot in Sandacre Street is Barton No 1213 (LAL 315K), a Plaxton-bodied Leyland PSU3B/4R new in May 1972. It was sold to Gilchrist of East Kilbride in November 1978, resold to Whitelaw of Bearsden in July 1980, and had passed to Hogg of Bearsden by April 1984.

The day before this view was taken the QE2 began its first round-the-world cruise, departing from New York City.

LEICESTER In St Margarets bus station is Midland Red No 5345 (6345 HA), a BMMO D9 that was new in October 1963 and spent much of its service life in Leicester before being retired in July 1977.

On this day Soyuz 17 carried two cosmonauts to the space station Salyut 4. They became the first men to occupy it, and returned to Earth on 7 February after setting a new record for the most days – 28 – spent in outer space.

LEICESTER Working a Park and Ride service in Burleys Way is Leicester No 209 (ARY 209K), an MCW-bodied Scania BR111MH new in November 1971. Unlike the case with a number of operators that used early Scanias, Leicester's were quite long-lived. No 209 was involved in an accident in May 1986, cannibalised for spares and scrapped in March 1987.

LEICESTER Allocated to Leicester for its entire service life was Midland Red No 6088 (JHA 88E), an Alexander-bodied Daimler CRG6LX new in July 1967 and withdrawn from service in August 1978. It was photographed in St Margarets bus station on 11 January.

A few days later, after a run of eight seasons, NBC broadcast the 199th and final episode of Ironside, starring Raymond Burr as wheelchair-bound police detective Robert Ironside.

LEICESTER Between May and August 1958 Leicester took delivery of 12 Leyland PD3/1s, Nos 161 to 172 (TBC 161 to 172); Nos 161 to 163 were bodied by Park Royal, 164 to 166 had Willowbrook bodywork, and 167 to 172 had bodywork by MCCW. This is Park Royal-bodied No 161 on service 18; a few days later it was withdrawn and sold to Pearson of Hetton-le-Hole, where it remained until scrapped in July 1980.

The excellent Status Quo were at No 1 in the singles chart with Down Down.

1975 TV Favourites a selection

Celebrity Squares (ATV/ITV)
Bob Monkhouse hosted game show first of initial run of 138 episodes broadcast in July

Dad's Army (BBC)
The eighth series of 6 episodes plus a Christmas special of the popular look at life in The Home Guard

Doctor Who (BBC)
Tom Baker, the fourth Doctor, encounters the birth of the Daleks amongst the year's adventures.

Fawlty Towers (BBC)
The start of the legendary shows starring John Cleese, Prunella Scales, Andrew Sachs and Connie Booth.

The Sweeney (ABC)
The first episode *Ringer* transmits on 2 January

The Naked Civil Servant (ITV)
Screened on 17 December, this 85 minute film of the life of Quentin Crisp, played by John Hurt, took the nation by storm winning a Best Actor BAFTA for John Hurt. .

Above: **CHELTENHAM** In March 1974 Black & White Motorways took delivery of 12 Duple-bodied Leyland PSU3B/4Rs, Nos 100 to 111 (PDD 100M to 111M), and standing in Cheltenham coach station on 26 April is No 105 (PDD 105M).

A few days earlier William Hartnell, who had been the first Doctor Who from 1963 to 1966, died in Kent at the age of 67.

Above right: **CHELTENHAM** Working a local service is No 8538 (993 EHW), an ECW-bodied Bristol LD6G new to Bristol in October 1959. In February 1977 it became driver trainer No W166, then passed firstly to Cheltenham & Gloucester in September 1983, and two months later to Midland Red North, still as a driver trainer, by this time 24 years old.

In the Top 20 album charts in January – and in my collection of vinyl at that time – were Straight Shooter (Bad Company), Tubular Bells (Mike Oldfield), Young Americans (David Bowie), Rubycon (Tangerine Dream) and Crime of the Century (Supertramp). I might add that I still have these vinyl albums, cherished to this day.

LONDON Transport was not an early convert to the Leyland National. It had made a large commitment to single-decker operation in the shape of hundreds of Merlins and Swifts, but they were not proving trouble-free. It therefore authorised a trial using six dual-door short Nationals and six dual-door MS Class Metro-Scanias. The Nationals joined the Metro-Scanias at Dalston Garage in November 1973 for route S2. They carried a deep red livery, with white roofs and grey pods, and seen in this livery on 11 October is No LS5 (TGY 105M). It was sold in May 1985 to British Airtours and was operated at Belfast Airport until May 1997, when it was acquired for preservation.

ROMFORD London Country RCLs were 30-foot Routemaster Park Royal-bodied coaches, and were developed from the RMC coaches, sharing their style. To maintain performance, 11.3-litre AEC AV690 engines were fitted, driving through semi-automatic gearboxes and high-ratio gears, and they were quick. In Romford heading for Tilbury Ferry is RCL No 2246 (CUV 246C), new in 1965. By the time this view was taken on 11 October it had been downgraded to a bus. It was purchased by London Transport in June 1979, the doors removed and seats refitted; it re-entered service on the 149 in June 1980, and remained there until withdrawal and sale in October 1983.

ROMFORD British European Airways had long operated a service between its London terminal and Heathrow Airport for domestic and European passengers. This had started in the 1950s with half-decker Commer Commandos, and continued with a dedicated fleet of BEA RFs. In the mid-1960s it was time for replacements to be ordered, and BEA conducted trials with double-deckers, one a very ugly AEC Regent V with a large rear luggage compartment, and the other RMF No 1254 with a trailer. The RMF trials were successful, and BEA ordered a fleet of 65, together with 88 trailers. By 1975 13 of them were deemed redundant and were sold to London Transport in August for £3,000 each. Their forward entrances, doors, high gearing and semi-automatic gearboxes made them unsuitable for City work, but a niche was identified on the 175 between Dagenham and North Romford. They went into service on that route in early October 1975, but were not very popular. The lack of internal stanchions was a drawback for both staff and passengers, while the lack of destination information was also a nuisance. Seen in Romford on 11 October is No RMA9 (NMY 646E); in this view it can be seen that the towing hook has been removed.